2008 POCKET DI

Austr
Birds

PERSONAL DETAILS

Name

Address

Postcode

Phone

Fax

Mobile

E-mail

www.steveparish.com.au

2008 School Holidays

VICTORIA
22 Dec 07 – 28 Jan 08
21 March – 6 April
28 June – 13 July
20 Sept – 5 Oct
20 Dec – 27 Jan 09

SOUTH AUSTRALIA
15 Dec 07 – 28 Jan 08
12 April – 27 April
5 July – 20 July
27 Sept – 12 Oct
13 Dec – 26 Jan 09

WESTERN AUSTRALIA
12 Dec 07 – 3 Feb 08
12 April – 27 April
5 July – 20 July
27 Sept – 12 Oct
17 Dec – 1 Feb 09

NORTHERN TERRITORY
15 Dec 07 – 29 Jan 08
5 April – 13 April
21 June – 20 July
27 Sept – 5 Oct
13 Dec – 27 Jan 09

QUEENSLAND
15 Dec 07 – 28 Jan 08
5 April – 14 April
28 June – 14 July
20 Sept – 5 Oct
13 Dec – 26 Jan 09

TASMANIA
21 Dec 07 – 13 Feb 08
25 March – 30 March
31 May – 15 June
6 Sept – 21 Sept
19 Dec – Feb 09

AUSTRALIAN CAPITAL TERRITORY
22 Dec 07 – 31 Jan 08
12 April – 27 April
5 July – 20 July
27 Sept – 12 Oct
20 Dec – 29 Jan 09

NEW SOUTH WALES
22 Dec 07 – 28 Jan 08
12 April – 27 April
5 July – 20 July
27 Sept – 12 Oct
20 Dec – 26 Jan 09

EASTER
21 March – 24 March

Please note: All information was correct on publication but is subject to change. Dates given are for State schools. Parents or carers should check with schools for pupil-free days each term.

WEEK 1

JANUARY

New Year's Day

Tuesday 1

Wednesday 2

Thursday 3

Friday 4

Saturday 5

Sunday 6

WEEK 2

JANUARY

Monday 7

NEW MOON

Tuesday 8

Wednesday 9

Thursday 10

Friday 11

Saturday 12

Sunday 13

Sulphur-crested Cockatoo, *Cacatua galerita*

JANUARY

WEEK 3

14 Monday

15 Tuesday

16 Wednesday

FIRST QUARTER

17 Thursday

18 Friday

19 Saturday

20 Sunday

WEEK 4

JANUARY

Monday 21

FULL MOON

Tuesday 22

Wednesday 23

Thursday 24

Friday 25

Australia Day

Saturday 26

Sunday 27

WEEK 5

JANUARY | FEBRUARY

Australia Day Holiday

Monday 28

Tuesday 29

LAST QUARTER

Wednesday 30

Thursday 31

Friday 1

Saturday 2

Sunday 3

Southern Cassowary, *Casuarius casuarius*

FEBRUARY

4 Monday

5 Tuesday

6 Wednesday

7 Thursday

Chinese New Year (Year of the Rat)

NEW MOON

8 Friday

9 Saturday

10 Sunday

WEEK 7

FEBRUARY

Monday 11

Tuesday 12

Wednesday 13

St Valentine's Day

FIRST QUARTER

Thursday 14

Friday 15

Saturday 16

Sunday 17

FEBRUARY

WEEK 8

18 Monday

19 Tuesday

20 Wednesday

21 Thursday

FULL MOON

22 Friday

23 Saturday

24 Sunday

Previous pages: Superb Lyrebird, *Menura novaehollandiae*

FEBRUARY | MARCH

Monday 25

Tuesday 26

Wednesday 27

Thursday 28

LAST QUARTER

Friday 29

Saturday 1

Sunday 2

MARCH

WEEK 10

3 Monday

Labour Day (WA)

4 Tuesday

5 Wednesday

6 Thursday

7 Friday

8 Saturday

NEW MOON

9 Sunday

Previous pages: Australian Pelican, *Pelecanus conspicillatus*

MARCH

Eight Hours Day (Tas); Labour Day (Vic); Adelaide Cup (SA)

Monday 10

Tuesday 11

Wednesday 12

Thursday 13

FIRST QUARTER

Friday 14

Saturday 15

Sunday 16

WEEK 12

MARCH

Canberra Day (ACT)

Monday 17

Tuesday 18

Wednesday 19

Thursday 20

Good Friday

Friday 21

Easter Saturday

FULL MOON

Saturday 22

Easter Sunday

Sunday 23

Peregrine Falcon, ***Falco peregrinus***

MARCH

WEEK 13

24 Monday

Easter Monday

25 Tuesday

Easter Tuesday (Tas)

26 Wednesday

27 Thursday

28 Friday

29 Saturday

30 Sunday

Daylight Saving ends (NSW, Vic, ACT, SA, Tas)

LAST QUARTER

WEEK 14

MARCH | APRIL

Monday 31

Tuesday 1

Wednesday 2

Thursday 3

Friday 4

Saturday 5

NEW MOON

Sunday 6

APRIL

WEEK 15

7 Monday

8 Tuesday

9 Wednesday

10 Thursday

11 Friday

12 Saturday

13 Sunday

FIRST QUARTER

Previous pages: Pacific Black Ducklings, *Anas superciliosa*

WEEK 16

APRIL

Monday 14

Tuesday 15

Wednesday 16

Thursday 17

Friday 18

Saturday 19

FULL MOON

Sunday 20

APRIL

Monday 21

Tuesday 22

Wednesday 23

Thursday 24

Anzac Day Holiday

Friday 25

Saturday 26

Sunday 27

Rainbow Bee-eater, *Merops ornatus*

APRIL | MAY

WEEK 18

28 Monday

29 Tuesday

LAST QUARTER

30 Wednesday

1 Thursday

2 Friday

3 Saturday

4 Sunday

WEEK 19

MAY

Labour Day (Qld); May Day (NT)

NEW MOON

Monday 5

Tuesday 6

Wednesday 7

Thursday 8

Friday 9

Saturday 10

Mother's Day

Sunday 11

MAY

WEEK 20

12 Monday

FIRST QUARTER

13 Tuesday

14 Wednesday

15 Thursday

16 Friday

17 Saturday

18 Sunday

Previous pages: **Crimson Chat, *Epthianura tricolor***

WEEK 21

MAY

Monday 19

FULL MOON

Tuesday 20

Wednesday 21

Thursday 22

Friday 23

Saturday 24

Sunday 25

MAY | JUNE

WEEK 22

26 Monday

27 Tuesday

28 Wednesday

LAST QUARTER

29 Thursday

30 Friday

31 Saturday

1 Sunday

Previous pages: Superb Fairy-wrens, *Malurus cyaneus*

WEEK 23

JUNE

Foundation Day (WA)

Monday 2

Tuesday 3

NEW MOON

Wednesday 4

Thursday 5

Friday 6

Saturday 7

Sunday 8

WEEK 24

JUNE

Queen's Birthday Holiday (All States except WA)

Monday 9

Tuesday 10

FIRST QUARTER

Wednesday 11

Thursday 12

Friday 13

Saturday 14

Sunday 15

Plumed Whistling-Duck, *Dendrocygna eytoni*

JUNE

WEEK 25

16 Monday

17 Tuesday

18 Wednesday

19 Thursday

FULL MOON

20 Friday

21 Saturday

22 Sunday

Monday 23

Tuesday 24

Wednesday 25

LAST QUARTER

Thursday 26

Friday 27

Saturday 28

Sunday 29

WEEK 27

JUNE | JULY

Monday 30

Tuesday 1

Wednesday 2

NEW MOON

Thursday 3

Friday 4

Saturday 5

Sunday 6

Australian Pelican, *Pelecanus conspicillatus*

JULY

WEEK 28

7 Monday

8 Tuesday

9 Wednesday

10 Thursday

FIRST QUARTER

11 Friday

12 Saturday

13 Sunday

JULY

Monday 14

Tuesday 15

Wednesday 16

Thursday 17

FULL MOON

Friday 18

Saturday 19

Sunday 20

JULY

WEEK 30

21 Monday

22 Tuesday

23 Wednesday

24 Thursday

25 Friday

26 Saturday

LAST QUARTER

27 Sunday

Previous pages: Scarlet Robin, *Petroica multicolor*

WEEK 31

JULY | AUGUST

Monday 28

Tuesday 29

Wednesday 30

Thursday 31

NEW MOON

Friday 1

Saturday 2

Sunday 3

WEEK 32

AUGUST

Picnic Day (NT); Bank Holiday (NSW)

Monday 4

Tuesday 5

Wednesday 6

Thursday 7

Friday 8

FIRST QUARTER

Saturday 9

Sunday 10

Regent Bowerbird, ***Sericulus chrysocephalus***

AUGUST

WEEK 33

11 Monday

12 Tuesday

13 Wednesday

People's Day, Royal Queensland Show (Brisbane)

14 Thursday

15 Friday

16 Saturday

17 Sunday

FULL MOON

WEEK 34

AUGUST

Monday 18

Tuesday 19

Wednesday 20

Thursday 21

Friday 22

Saturday 23

LAST QUARTER

Sunday 24

WEEK 35

AUGUST

Monday 25

Tuesday 26

Wednesday 27

Thursday 28

Friday 29

Saturday 30

NEW MOON

Sunday 31

Gouldian Finch, ***Erythrura gouldiae***

SEPTEMBER

WEEK 36

1 Monday

2 Tuesday

3 Wednesday

4 Thursday

5 Friday

6 Saturday

7 Sunday

Father's Day

WEEK 37

SEPTEMBER

FIRST QUARTER

Monday 8

Tuesday 9

Wednesday 10

Thursday 11

Friday 12

Saturday 13

Sunday 14

WEEK 38

SEPTEMBER

FULL MOON

Monday 15

Tuesday 16

Wednesday 17

Thursday 18

Friday 19

Saturday 20

Sunday 21

Galah, *Cacatua roseicapilla*

SEPTEMBER

WEEK 39

22 Monday

LAST QUARTER

23 Tuesday

24 Wednesday

25 Thursday

26 Friday

27 Saturday

28 Sunday

WEEK 40 SEPTEMBER | OCTOBER

Queen's Birthday (WA)

NEW MOON

Monday 29

Tuesday 30

Wednesday 1

Thursday 2

Friday 3

Saturday 4

Daylight Saving begins (Tas)

Sunday 5

OCTOBER

WEEK 41

6 Monday

Labour Day (ACT, NSW, SA)

7 Tuesday

FIRST QUARTER

8 Wednesday

9 Thursday

10 Friday

11 Saturday

12 Sunday

Previous pages: Emu, *Dromaius novaehollandiae*

WEEK 42

OCTOBER

Monday 13

Tuesday 14

FULL MOON

Wednesday 15

Thursday 16

Friday 17

Saturday 18

Sunday 19

WEEK 43

OCTOBER

Monday 20

LAST QUARTER

Tuesday 21

Wednesday 22

Thursday 23

Friday 24

Saturday 25

Daylight Saving begins (NSW, Vic, ACT, SA)

Sunday 26

Spinifex Pigeon, *Geophaps plumifera*

OCTOBER | NOVEMBER

WEEK 44

27 Monday

28 Tuesday

29 Wednesday

NEW MOON

30 Thursday

31 Friday

1 Saturday

2 Sunday

WEEK 45

NOVEMBER

Recreation Day (Northern Tas)

Monday 3

Melbourne Cup (Melbourne)

Tuesday 4

Wednesday 5

FIRST QUARTER

Thursday 6

Friday 7

Saturday 8

Sunday 9

NOVEMBER

WEEK 46

10 Monday

11 Tuesday

Remembrance Day

12 Wednesday

13 Thursday

FULL MOON

14 Friday

15 Saturday

16 Sunday

Previous pages: Black-faced Cormorants, *Halacrocorax fuscescens,* and a Pacific Gull, *Larus pacificus*

WEEK 47

NOVEMBER

Monday 17

Tuesday 18

Wednesday 19

LAST QUARTER

Thursday 20

Friday 21

Saturday 22

Sunday 23

NOVEMBER

WEEK 48

24 Monday

25 Tuesday

26 Wednesday

27 Thursday

28 Friday

NEW MOON

29 Saturday

30 Sunday

Previous pages: Laughing Kookaburra, *Dacelo novaeguineae*

WEEK 49

DECEMBER

Monday 1

Tuesday 2

Wednesday 3

Thursday 4

Friday 5

FIRST QUARTER

Saturday 6

Sunday 7

WEEK 50

DECEMBER

Monday 8

Tuesday 9

Wednesday 10

Thursday 11

Friday 12

FULL MOON

Saturday 13

Sunday 14

Crimson Rosella, *Platycercus elegans elegans*

DECEMBER

WEEK 51

15 Monday

16 Tuesday

17 Wednesday

18 Thursday

19 Friday

LAST QUARTER

20 Saturday

21 Sunday

DECEMBER

Monday 22

Tuesday 23

Wednesday 24

Christmas Day

Thursday 25

Boxing Day; Proclamation Day (SA)

Friday 26

NEW MOON

Saturday 27

Sunday 28

DECEMBER

29 Monday

30 Tuesday

31 Wednesday

Addresses

NAME

ADDRESS

P/CODE

PHONE (HOME) (WORK)

MOBILE FAX

E-MAIL

NAME

ADDRESS

P/CODE

PHONE (HOME) (WORK)

MOBILE FAX

E-MAIL

NAME

ADDRESS

P/CODE

PHONE (HOME) (WORK)

MOBILE FAX

E-MAIL

NAME

ADDRESS

P/CODE

PHONE (HOME) (WORK)

MOBILE FAX

E-MAIL

NAME

ADDRESS

P/CODE

PHONE (HOME) (WORK)

MOBILE FAX

E-MAIL

Addresses

NAME

ADDRESS

P/CODE

PHONE (HOME) (WORK)

MOBILE FAX

E-MAIL

NAME

ADDRESS

P/CODE

PHONE (HOME) (WORK)

MOBILE FAX

E-MAIL

NAME

ADDRESS

P/CODE

PHONE (HOME) (WORK)

MOBILE FAX

E-MAIL

NAME

ADDRESS

P/CODE

PHONE (HOME) (WORK)

MOBILE FAX

E-MAIL

NAME

ADDRESS

P/CODE

PHONE (HOME) (WORK)

MOBILE FAX

E-MAIL

Addresses

NAME

ADDRESS

P/CODE

PHONE (HOME) (WORK)

MOBILE FAX

E-MAIL

NAME

ADDRESS

P/CODE

PHONE (HOME) (WORK)

MOBILE FAX

E-MAIL

NAME

ADDRESS

P/CODE

PHONE (HOME) (WORK)

MOBILE FAX

E-MAIL

NAME

ADDRESS

P/CODE

PHONE (HOME) (WORK)

MOBILE FAX

E-MAIL

NAME

ADDRESS

P/CODE

PHONE (HOME) (WORK)

MOBILE FAX

E-MAIL

NOTES

2008

JANUARY

M	T	W	T	F	S	S
	1	2	3	4	5	6
7	8	9	10	11	12	13
14	15	16	17	18	19	20
21	22	23	24	25	26	27
28	29	30	31			

FEBRUARY

M	T	W	T	F	S	S
				1	2	3
4	5	6	7	8	9	10
11	12	13	14	15	16	17
18	19	20	21	22	23	24
25	26	27	28	29		

MARCH

M	T	W	T	F	S	S
31					1	2
3	4	5	6	7	8	9
10	11	12	13	14	15	16
17	18	19	20	21	22	23
24	25	26	27	28	29	30

APRIL

M	T	W	T	F	S	S
	1	2	3	4	5	6
7	8	9	10	11	12	13
14	15	16	17	18	19	20
21	22	23	24	25	26	27
28	29	30				

MAY

M	T	W	T	F	S	S
			1	2	3	4
5	6	7	8	9	10	11
12	13	14	15	16	17	18
19	20	21	22	23	24	25
26	27	28	29	30	31	

JUNE

M	T	W	T	F	S	S
30						1
2	3	4	5	6	7	8
9	10	11	12	13	14	15
16	17	18	19	20	21	22
23	24	25	26	27	28	29

JULY

M	T	W	T	F	S	S
	1	2	3	4	5	6
7	8	9	10	11	12	13
14	15	16	17	18	19	20
21	22	23	24	25	26	27
28	29	30	31			

AUGUST

M	T	W	T	F	S	S
				1	2	3
4	5	6	7	8	9	10
11	12	13	14	15	16	17
18	19	20	21	22	23	24
25	26	27	28	29	30	31

SEPTEMBER

M	T	W	T	F	S	S
1	2	3	4	5	6	7
8	9	10	11	12	13	14
15	16	17	18	19	20	21
22	23	24	25	26	27	28
29	30					

OCTOBER

M	T	W	T	F	S	S
		1	2	3	4	5
6	7	8	9	10	11	12
13	14	15	16	17	18	19
20	21	22	23	24	25	26
27	28	29	30	31		

NOVEMBER

M	T	W	T	F	S	S
					1	2
3	4	5	6	7	8	9
10	11	12	13	14	15	16
17	18	19	20	21	22	23
24	25	26	27	28	29	30

DECEMBER

M	T	W	T	F	S	S
1	2	3	4	5	6	7
8	9	10	11	12	13	14
15	16	17	18	19	20	21
22	23	24	25	26	27	28
29	30	31				

2009

JANUARY

M	T	W	T	F	S	S
			1	2	3	4
5	6	7	8	9	10	11
12	13	14	15	16	17	18
19	20	21	22	23	24	25
26	27	28	29	30	31	

FEBRUARY

M	T	W	T	F	S	S
						1
2	3	4	5	6	7	8
9	10	11	12	13	14	15
16	17	18	19	20	21	22
23	24	25	26	27	28	

MARCH

M	T	W	T	F	S	S
30	31					1
2	3	4	5	6	7	8
9	10	11	12	13	14	15
16	17	18	19	20	21	22
23	24	25	26	27	28	29

APRIL

M	T	W	T	F	S	S
		1	2	3	4	5
6	7	8	9	10	11	12
13	14	15	16	17	18	19
20	21	22	23	24	25	26
27	28	29	30			

MAY

M	T	W	T	F	S	S
				1	2	3
4	5	6	7	8	9	10
11	12	13	14	15	16	17
18	19	20	21	22	23	24
25	26	27	28	29	30	31

JUNE

M	T	W	T	F	S	S
1	2	3	4	5	6	7
8	9	10	11	12	13	14
15	16	17	18	19	20	21
22	23	24	25	26	27	28
29	30					

JULY

M	T	W	T	F	S	S
		1	2	3	4	5
6	7	8	9	10	11	12
13	14	15	16	17	18	19
20	21	22	23	24	25	26
27	28	29	30	31		

AUGUST

M	T	W	T	F	S	S
31					1	2
3	4	5	6	7	8	9
10	11	12	13	14	15	16
17	18	19	20	21	22	23
24	25	26	27	28	29	30

SEPTEMBER

M	T	W	T	F	S	S
	1	2	3	4	5	6
7	8	9	10	11	12	13
14	15	16	17	18	19	20
21	22	23	24	25	26	27
28	29	30				

OCTOBER

M	T	W	T	F	S	S
			1	2	3	4
5	6	7	8	9	10	11
12	13	14	15	16	17	18
19	20	21	22	23	24	25
26	27	28	29	30	31	

NOVEMBER

M	T	W	T	F	S	S
30						1
2	3	4	5	6	7	8
9	10	11	12	13	14	15
16	17	18	19	20	21	22
23	24	25	26	27	28	29

DECEMBER

M	T	W	T	F	S	S
	1	2	3	4	5	6
7	8	9	10	11	12	13
14	15	16	17	18	19	20
21	22	23	24	25	26	27
28	29	30	31			

2010

JANUARY

M	T	W	T	F	S	S
				1	2	3
4	5	6	7	8	9	10
11	12	13	14	15	16	17
18	19	20	21	22	23	24
25	26	27	28	29	30	31

FEBRUARY

M	T	W	T	F	S	S
1	2	3	4	5	6	7
8	9	10	11	12	13	14
15	16	17	18	19	20	21
22	23	24	25	26	27	28

MARCH

M	T	W	T	F	S	S
1	2	3	4	5	6	7
8	9	10	11	12	13	14
15	16	17	18	19	20	21
22	23	24	25	26	27	28
29	30	31				

APRIL

M	T	W	T	F	S	S
			1	2	3	4
5	6	7	8	9	10	11
12	13	14	15	16	17	18
19	20	21	22	23	24	25
26	27	28	29	30		

MAY

M	T	W	T	F	S	S
31					1	2
3	4	5	6	7	8	9
10	11	12	13	14	15	16
17	18	19	20	21	22	23
24	25	26	27	28	29	30

JUNE

M	T	W	T	F	S	S
	1	2	3	4	5	6
7	8	9	10	11	12	13
14	15	16	17	18	19	20
21	22	23	24	25	26	27
28	29	30				

JULY

M	T	W	T	F	S	S
			1	2	3	4
5	6	7	8	9	10	11
12	13	14	15	16	17	18
19	20	21	22	23	24	25
26	27	28	29	30	31	

AUGUST

M	T	W	T	F	S	S
30	31					1
2	3	4	5	6	7	8
9	10	11	12	13	14	15
16	17	18	19	20	21	22
23	24	25	26	27	28	29

SEPTEMBER

M	T	W	T	F	S	S
		1	2	3	4	5
6	7	8	9	10	11	12
13	14	15	16	17	18	19
20	21	22	23	24	25	26
27	28	29	30			

OCTOBER

M	T	W	T	F	S	S
				1	2	3
4	5	6	7	8	9	10
11	12	13	14	15	16	17
18	19	20	21	22	23	24
25	26	27	28	29	30	31

NOVEMBER

M	T	W	T	F	S	S
1	2	3	4	5	6	7
8	9	10	11	12	13	14
15	16	17	18	19	20	21
22	23	24	25	26	27	28
29	30					

DECEMBER

M	T	W	T	F	S	S
		1	2	3	4	5
6	7	8	9	10	11	12
13	14	15	16	17	18	19
20	21	22	23	24	25	26
27	28	29	30	31		

Steve Parish has travelled Australia for over 40 years, portraying the marvels of this continent — its people, its cities, and its unique and beautiful landscapes, plants and animals — with the sensitivity and artistry that make him one of Australia's most celebrated photographers. Steve's passion for Australia, and his awareness that urgent human action is needed to preserve Australia's wild places and wild creatures, lends intensity to his work. He founded Steve Parish Publishing Pty Ltd to share his vision of Australia with the world.

Front cover: Laughing Kookaburra, *Dacelo novaeguineae*

PO Box 1058, Archerfield, Queensland 4108 Australia
Prepress by Colour Chiefs Digital Imaging, Brisbane, Australia
Printed in China by Compass Press
Produced at the Steve Parish Publishing Studios, Australia

www.steveparish.com.au

Steve Parish™
PUBLISHING
PROUDLY AUSTRALIAN OWNED